Uncensored Songs

For Sam Abrams

SPUYTEN DUYVIL

New York City

Edited by John Roche

Cover design by Tod Thilleman; cover photo by Greg Slater; portrait of Sam Abrams on back cover (also on p. 16) by Glenn Bewley; photograph on title page is *Preparation* by Diane Katsiaficas. Portrait of Sam Abrams on page 79 is by John Retallack. Other photos are by Diane Katsiaficas.

Note on back cover photo:
LeRoi Jones (later Amiri Baraka) on the stoop of his parents' home in East Orange, NJ, Summer 1959. Left to Right: Baraka's mother Anna behind the pillar, Baraka, Max Finstein, Tony Weinberger, Rena Oppenheimer holding Daniel, Hettie Jones holding Kelly, Joel Oppenheimer holding Nicholas, Elias Tsiimpadros, Elsene Sorrentino, Gil and Jesse Sorrentino, Sam Abrams. Photographer unknown.

This collection made possible by the friends of Sam Abrams. Any profits will be donated to the A.J. MUSTE MEMORIAL INSTITUTE. Supporting Nonviolence and Social Justice Since 1974: http://www.ajmuste.org/

This book was made possible by the generosity of the following individuals: Alan Boegehold, Jerry and Judith Abrams, Richard Fasse and Jean Douthwright, Joe Flaherty and Elizabeth Scott, Graham Mackenzie, Brenda Wenzel, Dennis Gettman, Mark Maslow, Larry Belle, Karen Fields, Joe Early, and John Roche.

Thanks to Paulette Swartzfager for help in reviewing this manuscript.

Portions of the following poems appeared in the special Sam Abrams Tribute in *Cadillac Cicatrix*, issue 1, Spring 2007: Andrei Codrescu, "With Love"; Jim Cohn, "Respondez!"; Bob Holman, "Praise"; Ed Sanders, "November 2005"; Michael Gregory Stephens, "A Sonnet" (as well as photographs by Diane Katsiaficas).

copyright 2008 All Rights Revert to Authors Upon Publication
ISBN 978-1-933132-55-6

Back cover: porch photograph
by Larry Hellenberg

This tribute anthology began on the occasion of Sam Abrams' retirement from Rochester Institute of Technology, where he taught for three decades, and also advised the student magazine, *Signatures*. As Sam had been granted Emeritus Professor status, we hoped to publish through RIT's Cary Press, but that proved impossible due to official disapproval—fortunately a new, more enlightened administration has taken office in recent weeks. Thanks to Mick Stephens for suggesting Spuyten Duyvil, and to Tod Thilleman for offering to publish this volume, and doing a superb job on the design. Thanks as well to Benjamin Spencer, whose moving tribute to Sam, which included excerpts from some of the poems in this volume, appeared in *Cadillac Cicatrix*, issue one, Sp 2007, cadillaccicatrix.com.

Sam Abrams embodies the notion that all poetry, like all politics, is local. He has left his mark on the many places he has lived and worked and struggled for peace and the right to free expression. The organization of this collection of works by his friends, students, and colleagues is roughly geographical (as well as chronological), beginning with his time in New York City in the 1960s, where he taught in the St. Mark's Poetry Project, engaged in agitprop with the Angry Arts Collective, and was a visible figure in the very exciting Lower East Side poetry scene. The volume moves to Greece (where the Abrams often winter), England, and elsewhere, before moving to Rochester, NY, which Sam and Barbara Abrams have called home for the past three decades.

The Purpose
—Sam Abrams

the purpose

of that cute little tailwag
robin does right after
perching on bare branch

is

to save & shake our world
as any fool old pothead
can plainly see

From The Old Pothead Poems

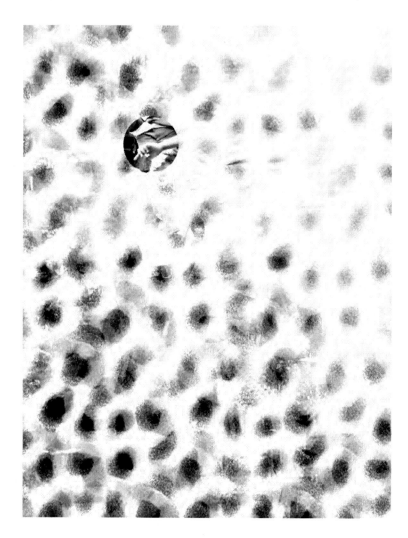

Haiku
—Vivianna Calabria

Sam gave me my first and only A+++++++++
(A with 10 pluses) for this two-person performance
Haiku:

"Take your order, ma'am?"
"Yes, I'd like a hell sandwich:
Fire between bread!"

I Hear it was Charged against Me
–Walt Whitman

I HEAR it was charged against me that I sought to destroy
    institutions;
But really I am neither for nor against institutions;
(What indeed have I in common with them?—Or what with
    the destruction of them?)
Only I will establish in the Mannahatta, and in every city of
    These States, inland and seaboard,
And in the fields and woods, and above every keel, little or
    large, that dents the water,
Without edifices, or rules, or trustees, or any argument,
The institution of the dear love of comrades.

From **America: A Prophecy**
—William Blake

Let the slave grinding at the mill, run out into the field:
Let him look up into the heavens & laugh in the bright air;
Let the inchained soul shut up in darkness and in sighing,
Whose face has never seen a smile in thirty weary years;
Rise and look out, his chains are loose, his dungeon
                                        doors are open.
And let his wife and children return from the opressors
                                        scourge;
They look behind at every step & believe it is a dream.
Singing. The Sun has left his blackness, & has found a
                                        fresher morning
And the fair Moon rejoices in the clear & cloudless night;
For Empire is no more, and now the Lion & Wolf shall cease.

Verse Preface
—John Roche

The Technoversity decreed
a stately sculpture of bronze, weathering steel,
                               and stainless steel
110 ton, 73-ft high
ploughshares turned into swords after 9/11
The Sentinel looms o'er the campus
like Clark Kerr's gates to the Multiversity—
a declaration of our mission, to be the shock-troops
                                       of cyberwar
(no hyperbole here)

The Prez of RIT decreed
not a penny shall be spent
honoring Sam-I-am,
noted incendiary and avowed Old Pothead
who gave Karma Points to students
was the bane of all administrators
and helped expose the canker on the former Presidency
(sick Rose's CIA skullduggery, with RIT craftsmen
building desks with hidden compartments—oh invisible worm!
—or designing digital imaging for the spy satellites
                               and the death drones)

So we publish these odes off-campus,
                         while speech is still possible
so long as patriots act

(And so Sam sang of the Secret Six,
and even cajoled the NY State Legislature to decree
Jan. 29, 2007 *Tom Paine Day*)

Praise Sonnet for Sam Abrams
—Bob Holman

Sam Abrams, Sam Abrams the song is on your head
Like a bullet for a hat, an irreplaceable book screen
There is no one in your DEA jacket, and the police
                                                    at the door
There is a wonderment though you are stepping through

By the bullshit of your tie and spittled joint
I will be a poet like you, if you don't mind
When you performed as Rimbaud at the Nuyorican
I knew there was a heaven and we were living it

Still, in spite of you, things go wrong
That's the purpose, Boss, of song as lid
The tightness of your drama has us in stitches
Datgummit! Rochester is snoring again, tra la

Sam Abrams, Sam Abrams, your unassuming wisdom
A course of poetry and politics that informs the Earth

for sam abrams with love
—andrei codrescu

the most imposing door
I have ever known a poet to have
across the street from St. marks' church
and it was opened by the namesake
of sam's novel
barbara herself
and I found myself at twenty years of age
a longhaired romanian
in the home of the greatest
new yorkers possible as if all that
eastern european jewish immigration
for the past one hundred years
had been for a very good purpose indeed
and when later I embarked on my education
by looking up the poetry classes
at the old courthouse on 2nd avenue
I settled for joel oppenheimer's instead
of sam abrams' because quote
in sam's class you have to smoke a joint
before class even starts unquote
i'm not sure who said that
maybe michael stephens who attended
sam's class though maybe just for the pot
but pot made me very nervous
still does
but hail the pot poet he's wise still
and you can get high just saying his name
sam abrams from new york poet

To Sam Abrams, 11/05
—Ed Sanders

Sam Abrams
old pal

always willing
to share your wisdom

& lists of books to read

Pal of the Revolution
of Peace, Freedom & Sharing

that will surely come
if not for the
mammals
    of our time on
    Gaia

Stand up, Sam!
so that we can toss some petals
from the Universal Rose

upon your brow!

I Am an Artist for Art's Sake

Tune: Eekh Bin Ah Boarder By Mine Vibe (Yiddish Song)
—Tuli Kupferberg

I am an Artist for Art's Sake
And it was God who gave me my Big Break
Told Me: "You were meant for a higher purpose—
To sweep the Stables of Pegasus!"
I am an Artist for Art's Sake.

Born with a Silver Ballroom in my mouth
A scion of the Olde Plantationist South
When other kids went out to work
What I did was sketch, pout, and shirk
I am an Artist for Art's Sake.

I believe in *Beauty* and *Truth*
Specially my beauty (and *your* Vermouth)
While other painters might join the Picket
I just cry: "Sticky wicket!"
I am an Artist for Art's Sake.

Hey! I'm also a Poet for Poetry's sake
(Ya can bet I'm a poet oney for Poetry's sake)
when other poets are in the street
I stay home and count my feet
I am a poet for Putz sake!

And I'm a musician for The Muses sake
{*other voice off*} "You're a musician for whosis sake?"
Well I do sit to a different drum
And my thumb up my bum makes a wonderful hum
I'm a Musician for A*muse*ments sake.

And I'm a writer for Royalties sake
I know it is *sales* that make or break
And I don't write for little presses
It's EAT or BE EATEN (and I'm a BIG FRESSER!)
I am a writer for my Publisher's sake.

And I am a journalist for the Owner's sake
(It's not exactly that I'm on the take)
But why write what the Editor don't like...
When there's 50 Cubs coming right down the pike?
I am a Reporter for the Advertiser's sake.

Surely there are more important things
Than Africa or the price of beans
I'll explore my Inner Space
(And I can't stand your Peasant face!)
I am an Artist for Art's sake.

Oh I do let the world pass me right by
(The Golden Section runs right thru my eye)
Let other people freeze and fight
Someone's got to *Paint it Right!*
I am an Artist for Art's Sake.

I am an Artist for Art's Sake
Twas God who gave me my big break
I was born for a Higher Reason
And all His angels I am pleasing
(spoken): I'm an *Artist* for *God's Sake!*

(NB: one may include spoken improv here on a current situation)

My Damp Pants, My Darling
for Sam
—Bob Rixon

Someone nailed
a White Castle burger
to the bulletin board.
It stayed there
for two semesters.

I could have learned
a lot in that time.

A Garland of Sonnets for Sam Abrams
—Mick Stephens

THE CHIEF EXECUTIVE

Dear God, relieve me of bureaucrats, these
Fat cats, tieless, in Oxford blue shirt sleeves,
All business, no nonsense, and full of
Crap, they come in on a Monday, leave us
On a Friday, with a mountain of work
To sort out by business next week, papers
Colour-coded, stacked refrigerator-
High, alphabetised, number-date crated.

You want to shout at them to disappear,
Take their piles and labeled portfolios,
And kiss off, really screw off, you want to
Say, take your crunched numbers, your green tally
Sheets, your pink and yellow tabs, brown shoes,
                                                                         red
Socks, and quite simply, beat it, scram, fuck off!

NELSON'S WATCH

Nelson, he sd, and it was Trafalgar,
Not Waterloo, as I sd, too far in
From the sea, though I had meant that my train
Was pulling into the railway station.
Then I sd to my friend, his watch, I sd,
Whose watch? Nelson's, I sd, it's going up
For auction, perhaps you'd want to bid on
It, he sd, no, he did not want to buy
Nelson's or any watch, for that matter,
He had one-hundred-and-forty or so,
And wanted to cut back on them for now,
So many of them had stopped working, stopped
Being of any use to him, except
To take up space in his flat, tick-tick-tick.

THE BICYCLIST

The traffic sets like a stalled game of chess,
Cars packed one behind the other, horns honk,
Drivers shout profanities, but nothing
Moves, congestion everywhere, sirens
Go off, tempers flare up. It is just near
Four o'clock on a Thursday afternoon,
Smog settles over the city, grey and still,
The Thames moments away, Monet-like.

Into this clot in the artery of
The city comes a bicyclist, green
And red and yellow and even orange
On his jacket and shorts, helmet on head,
He sings a song, top of his lungs, alive,
Alive, he is nothing but that, and well.

SPARROWS

The sparrows disappeared from London, not
One of them seen for years, until right now.
Here is one at my feet, here another,
They feed on the seeds and breadcrumbs, bits of
Food left by the crows, pigeons and blackbirds,
Pecking away, here and there, silent as
Ghosts. I want to ask them where they have been,
And why did they stay away for so long.

Two weeks after the first wave of bombers,
The next flock of zealot, suicidal
Attackers descend again, three under
Us on the Tube, one on a bus going
From Hackney to nowhere. Why do they hate
Us? a benighted soul asks me today.

WE INFIDELS

As they sat in the Hallucinations
Of sunlight and desert, eating grape leaves
And figs, we Infidels followed Francis
Of Assisi into the mountains of
Italy, or we plotted Longitudes
And Latitudes of the Earth, in search of
A new route to China. We did believe
In Things, and the new Roman god of Bread
And Wine, of the Transubstantiation
On a Cross, for even the god of Love
Had been Harnessed to the land-grab Machine
Of War which the Romans perfected, and
Let's not forget the Inventions we brought
The world: pasta, pesto, Caesar, toilets.

A SONNET FOR SAM ABRAMS

Michael, you ungrateful Irish bastard,
What did you ever do for Sam Abrams,
Your Lower East Side poetry teacher,
The Poundian in the Poetry Project mix,
The one who knew that Make It New came from
A bathtub in Canto Fifty-three, day
By day, Tching prayed on the mountain, make
It new, while Sam Abrams shouted from roofs
In the East Village, day by day, go see
Dorothy Day, Michael, and make a peace
With your warring spirit and poetry,
Make energy rise out of you like steam.
And for this, and more, I'll be forever
Grateful to Sam, the poet and madman.

Firsts with Sam
—Joel Sloman

I met Sam in 1966 around the time I began working at the Poetry Project. He liked me and sort of took me under his wing. We walked up and down Second Avenue a few times. He took me to a pornographic movie at a theater on Second near 14th, I think. It was my first porno flick. The movie was awful. I remember a woman masturbating in bed while someone peeked at her through a door. I can't remember if this was the best part.

I also remember eating protose steak with him in a dairy restaurant on 14th.

During and after Angry Arts Week early in '67, we were in the group that organized the Poets' Caravan (I think that's what we called it), reading antiwar poems from a flat-bed truck in neighborhoods in Queens and Manhattan. Once when we were parked on Delancey St. we had to abandon the truck because of a bomb scare.

Our planning meetings were held in a room in the courthouse on Second and 2nd, now the Millennium Film building. One morning when we were gathering there before meeting the truck, Sam took me into the judge's chambers and shared a joint with me. It was my first dope experience.

Then there was the time we were on Second during the afternoon rush hour. Dense traffic moved downtown. Sam had brought a small paper bag with him from his apartment. Somewhere around 11th or 12th he stopped and looked around as if to see if anybody was looking our way. Then as stealthily as possible he threw the bag into the street and we continued walking. I found out later that the bag was filled with nails.

Since the early years Sam has been loyal to me. This and his respect for me were important constants through long periods when I didn't otherwise get much of either. He knew I had a lot to learn and his lessons were more significant than he probably realizes. I'm grateful.

La Vuelta de los Gusanos
—George Kimball

In the spring and summer of 1967, with the Vietnam war raging, Sam Abrams was instrumental in helping develop a program we called "Angry Arts Against the War." On weekend mornings we'd arrive, unannounced, at some busy location in the five boroughs, where unsuspecting passers-by would be treated to a few hours of anti-war flavored poetry, jazz and folk music, and, most weekends, an agit-prop performance by the Pageant Players, all enacted from a 'stage' — the rear of a flat-bed truck, equipped with a portable sound system borrowed from the Poetry Project at St. Mark's-in-the-Bowery — while other members of the troupe leafleted the crowd.

Procuring the truck itself was no mean feat. Four decades ago car-hire companies were extremely reluctant to rent to anyone perceived to be of the hippie persuasion, but we'd developed a system that seemed to work. We'd reserve the truck in advance, and each Saturday morning Joe Early and I would go over to pick it up (me because I had a chauffeur's license, Joe because in 1967 he was the only poet in New York in possession of an American Express card), then rendezvous with the others outside St. Mark's, and head off for our designated location.

Although Joel Sloman recalls a Saturday performance on Delancey Street being disrupted by a bomb scare, our audiences were for the most part respectful, if a bit bewildered. Sometimes they'd stop and listen for hours, but more often for a just a few minutes, before they moved on. Sometimes they'd ask questions, and occasionally one of them might even engage us in a spirited sidewalk debate.

One lovely Saturday morning that year we'd decided to take our message to Spanish Harlem. Early and I had collected the truck, after which Joe repaired to his headquarters — a barstool at Max's Kansas City — to nurse a hangover. I picked up Sam and the rest of the gang on Second Avenue, and we made our way uptown. (Nearly forty years later I'm not altogether certain who else might have been among that morning's crew, but some permutation from among the usual suspects — Sloman, Tony Weinberger, David Henderson, Larry Meyers, Dick Lourie, Clayton Eshleman, Fielding Dawson, Dan Georgakas, Gary Youree, and Art Berger — wouldn't be a bad guess.)

An hour or so into that day's performance the Angry Artists were attacked without warning by an even angrier mob which had suddenly materialized on the sidewalk before us. Confusion reigned. My recollection is that the Pageant Players were onstage at the time, and since most of them were in costume they couldn't even see what was going on until they started getting toppled like life-sized bowling pins. There were shouts and shrieks in at least two languages, missiles flying through the air, and, just below us, a hostile swarm of club-toting bodies trying to clamber onto the truck like a boarding party of bloodthirsty buccaneers.

Whatever audience we had accumulated quickly disappeared as most of them scattered and ran for cover. I was standing there on the back of the truck when I was decked. I went down like I'd been shot, slammed over backward from the impact, and while I wasn't quite knocked out, I did, literally, see stars. The next thing I knew Sam was dragging me to my feet and shouting at me to get back in the cab and get the truck out of there.

Since I hadn't seen my assailant I assumed I'd been felled by either a blindside hook worthy of Joe Frazier or an unopened can of beans fired from the sidewalk. Only later did Joe Early explain that I had been hit by a very expensive stand microphone (ours; it was subsequently recovered), which my assailant had presumably swung like a baseball bat. I was, in any case, bleeding like Chuck Wepner from a gash across my forehead, and barely conscious as Sam pushed me into the cab and told me to get the hell out of there.

This would have been a few years before Sam became a crack shot and a martial-arts expert, and in fact back in those days Sam wouldn't have ventured above 14th Street without getting himself ritualistically stoned beforehand. Knowing this, I was nearly as startled by his abrupt metamorphosis into a heightened state of coherency as I was at having been taken out by a rogue microphone.

I gunned the engine and somehow — blood was pouring into my one functional eye — we beat our hasty retreat.

Our escape was facilitated by a fortuitous convergence of events. Our assailants, it turned out, were a mob of Gusanos — expatriate Cuban anti-communists — led by a former colonel of Batista's secret police. As they set upon us, they had in turn been bravely confronted by a pair of outraged bystanders — a diminutive Columbia psychology professor and his even tinier wife. The Cubans were so shocked that they momentarily hesitated, giving me just enough time to fish the keys out of my pocket.

And then, just as we fired up the engine, the cavalry arrived to cover our strategic withdrawal. A gang comprised of the local Puerto Ricans on whose turf we had been performing waded into the Cubans, giving as good as they got, and we sped away from the scene a full-scale rumble raged behind us. The Puerto Rican kids, it turned out, harbored no strong feelings about either the Vietnam war or the first-amendment rights of poets. They just didn't like the Gusanos.

I guess I was the most visible casualty of the day, but while it bled a lot, once it was cleaned up my head wound wasn't much worse than some I'd had before and since, and by the time we returned to home base you'd have thought we'd actually won the skirmish.

I tried to thank Sam for saving my ass, but he confessed that it hadn't been my ass he was worried about. He'd already been thinking about having to going back to St. Mark's and explain to Joel Oppenheimer that the Poetry Project's sound system lay scattered in bits in front of some bodega up in Spanish Harlem.

Sam's response: I reject the canard about being more concerned about the sound system than George...we actually owned the sound system as I recall, but not the expensive mic; however, we can let that stand as fair exchange for my having to fetch George out of the bar where he was, in spite of my warning to stay close cause it looked like trouble...glued to the game on tv....i was terrified, as the wound was just above George's only real eye onto which blood was streaming...

I put on record at this time my great admiration for George's driving skills, he handled the big truck as if it were compact...and amazingly, as he demonstrated at out of town peace gigs like the DC mobilization, he could arrive in a city he hadn't been near for many years, and drive through it at high speed, never hesitate, and never make a wrong turn...if he ever loses his writing talent, he could be a champion hackie....

Tony Weinberger's response: Unlike the rest of us on the bed of the truck, Sam always wore the same academic uniform: soft shoes, baggy cotton slacks, an open-throated solid color Oxford button-downed shirt & a hound's tooth check black & white tweed sports jacket.

For a change we ventured over the 59th St. Bridge. One stop was at Queen's Village where the incident happened. Sam was reciting an anti-war poem before a restive crowd [Now we always kept a wary eye out for angry young men who might crack & jump us. But at this stop none of us anticipated where the antipathy would come from]. Suddenly, a house-frau in curlers & a scarf started screaming quite pointedly at Sam: "You damn hippies—why don't you go back where you came from—take a bath & shave!"

Do you remember what Sam looked like in those days? He would arrive so closely-shaven his face shone & his hair was still wet from his shower.

Letter from Larry Meyers:

Dear Sam,

I just read your resume and your pothead poems. I liked you better when you turned in your draft card at Whitehall and later thought you'd have to decamp to England. I liked you better on the beach in California when some bourgeois complained we were treading on his sand and you said he'd pay when his daughter grew up and found him odious. I liked you better when you gave me a pair of corduroys and pretended they didn't fit you. I even liked you better when I found a plaster cast of a classical figure on a midnight street and you wondered aloud how I rather than you, a trained scholar, could acquire that. I liked you better then because I liked everything better then, and because everything was better then, no matter how nostalgia exalts the past and downgrades the present as a matter of course

Your old comrade in arms,
Larry

Teacher
/For Sam
—Joe Early

writing
began
with
lists

we
were
forgetful

learned
a
tool

soared.

Sam "Respondez!" Abrams
—Jim Cohn

It wasn't hard to run into Sam. He could be found in solo weekly streetcorner antiwar vigil outside the Village Green Bookstore on Monroe Avenue in Rochester for anyone with a brain to ponder. Brains was the thing. Sam Abrams is a poet's poet—wired for action—on the page and in the sangha of the muse.

Sam embodied the white male card-carrying ACLU poet activist—raving, free-thinking, and audacious. An intelligencia ruffian, he always struck me as someone with a certain racy wild smack about him. I was like anybody that feels a definite warmth of affection toward certain people that others may find generally disagreeable or outright antagonistic.

Hanging out with Sam was like attending a highgrass course on the satori of protest. If poetry can be described as a form of sex between heaven and earth, Sam had the whole naked library in his head. If poetry is peace storming the battlefield, he would, in the battle of poetry, take the masters of war out of their graves and shoot them again, to paraphrase Amiri Baraka, with the facts lodged in the world they have oppressed.

I met Sam soon after moving to Rochester in 1982. He encouraged me to begin my first magazine, *Action*, a mimeo job, in 1983. I think we were at a reading by Philip Whalen. Snow was coming down fast and hard as it does in the Great Lakes Districts. Reagan was in the White House entertaining America with a unique blend of Hollywood and Dementia. Philip burned each poem after reading it. It was quite a remarkable performance. Philip was all or nothing in that way.

In the half-light of one of the most superb of evenings, I recall Sam turning to me to say something that seemed part Homer, Sappho and part Ted Berrigan: "Not by the imposition of any extension or disassociation or mythology or history, there's something happening here that a group wants to say." And he wasn't wrong about that. Although the post-Beat era corresponds to the widespread demise of the publishing counterculture, for Sam the best poesy productions take place in a local context that suggests the rugged hipster commune of verse will never die.

Sam turned me on to Paul Blackburn with his poem "Visiting Hours." He introduced me to Joel Oppenheimer. He was the St. Marks Poetry Project ambassador to Lake Ontario's shores. Unlike Bob Creeley down the road in Buffalo, with whom he enjoyed great friendship, Sam was our more hidden upstate master. Embodying differing phases of Objectivist and Black Mountain and New York School affinities than Creeley, Sam's was a more indeterminate voice—one that reflects the Civil Rights Soul of the American Experience.

Abrams will be remembered for two excellent versions of trickster cosmic consciousness. With a body of published work that is as freewheeling and investigative as Hunter Thompson, Edward Sanders, and Michael Moore, his prose book, *The Neglected Walt Whitman: Vital Texts* (Four Walls Eight Windows, 1993), reflects a scholarly rebellion against the wimp reactionary forces of well-funded and "authoritative" literary canon dullards. His overly slim volume of selected poems, *The Old Pothead Poems*, (Creative Arts, 2003), is at once classicist in its lyric, savage in its modernity, striking for the creative impulses that underlie its conceits, and informative for its sense that poems are not composed "in the head, but 'on the breath.'"

He accomplished this while holding down a faculty position teaching literature and poetry. One semester I was in his class—not as a student, but as a sign language interpreter. It wasn't pretty. You could only be stimulated by the burlesque of contemporary experimental poetry being taught without any attempt to "crack" it. And no matter how hard his students might want him to get at it or take it apart, he knew you just couldn't do that. So, it is no surprise that throughout his tenure as Professor of English at Rochester Institute of Technology, Sam was a digital age visionary, anticipating and rejecting the technomaterialism of intellectual property.

One of the ways he kept it together was having a special kinship with Allen Ginsberg. My most vivid contact with Sam centers on his bringing Allen to RIT in February 1984. During that visit, he invited me to add an event to Allen's already crammed itinerary that called for a panel discussion with Deaf poet Robert Panara. That meeting of Deaf and Beat poets—which featured a dialog on questions of translation related to the juxtapositional phrase "hydrogen jukebox" from "Howl"—resulted in a watershed for the advocacy of American Sign Language as a legitimate exemplary form of the American poetics canon.

One bitter cold night at Sam's Dartmouth Street home, I stopped by to interview Carl Rakosi. Sam and Barbara's generosity was always in attendance—good bread, good wine, good cheese, good dope. There was a bottle of 18-year-old single-malt scotch on the table that night and Carl was ready to talk about the thirty-year gap in his writing of poems. Rakosi was in his 80's when we met. He talked about Reznikoff and him being Marxists in the 1930s and how all the Communist journals and magazines would just annihilate poetry if it didn't have a social purpose. He talked about being boiled alive by the editors back then for pandering to the decadent taste of the bourgeoisie and how that was deadly to him and how that made him stop.

I know, for myself, I took something from Sam about how to get complex emotion and feeling down on the page in such a way as it may be gotten the first time and also make the reader come back a second time. I think of his poem, "Notes From The Plague Planet," and the following excerpt as an example:

30.13
In respect of the pain
they often say
the plague is a blessing
since it enables its "lucky" victims
to project onto an exterior agent
responsibility
for their sufferings.

Conversely the few
who escape the plague
often and bitterly complain
that the worst of the pain
is the inescapable knowledge
that it is self inflicted.

    Every time Sam wrote anything like that it's been a Big Door for me—unconscious enough to feed any reader in real-time spaces they may have to go and conscious enough to do everything that it does inclusively and casually enough and until the next one comes. Sam's place in U.S. poetics history is akin to that of Amiri Baraka and Jack Hirschman. He survived the pre and post Beat Generation era, an insurgent lynchpin spirit of revolutionary Samaritan populace justice. He survived the shifts in reporting environments that define and name the resistance forces.

3 December 2005

Open Field
for Sam Abrams
—Anne Waldman

       lexographic knowledge

          & gnosis of the senses
see! see!

words *do* complicate &

    retrieve the tributary   (sea! sea!)

detail, *the* political,
  plus poetic eccentricity (sexual)

philosophy gives caution to

   gone to make a man a *logopoeia* of resistance
     semblance

one man renaissance sounding

   through neighborhoods of Mediterranean light

     catches an eye

in gesture, demand, down home rhetorical
pleasures

  across the divide   (swirl)

whose? and what are the colors?

civilizations as economies we study   (mauve, dark purple)

   fire, writing, mathematics,   or stuff of dream
   the newest American poetry grammar

this kind of mind delves into

     mayhem = *leap*

Two Poems
—Alan L. Boegehold

A Member of the Academy

A rusty crow
across an orange
and setting sun
ravenous
flaps low
scavenging
pecking at bundles
deep in shadow
shrouded bulks
in lumpish rows
taking bits
for his gritty craw.

Looking Ahead

Old dog, silvery muzzle
lifts his head
when I put on my coat.
Heaven for him
is going to be
an endless walk
with me.

Knossos
−Karen E. Fields

In the summer of 1996, my daughter (Maïmouna) and I were visiting Barbara and Sam in Crete. We drove to Knossos one day and walked around with "Uncle Sam" the professor as our guide. He gave us the Rolls Royce of tours.

But Crete is hot in July, so I kept watching Maïmouna, only nine, for the signs you'd expect even if you're in the world of Theseus and the Minotaur. Sam kept walking, brisk as always and lecturing likewise despite the Cretan heat. Maïmouna was keeping up. Her Uncle Sam had on his funny hat and used his cane to indicate or else to punctuate his pearls of learning. He tapped with the cane and said, "Look! That stone dates from the Minoans." He stepped on it, "See how it's different from that one, put in later?" And so they zigzagged along, aiming to step on the Minoan stones: he, lecturing as from a podium and she, alert to learn what we do and don't know about the builders of the road she was traveling. Barbara and I fell back, the better to watch the peripatetic Sam Abrams at work.

The Endless Sea
—Benjamin Spencer

The sun breaks through large gray clouds and shines on Nea Hora beach. Barbara takes her shoes off and carries them in her hand. Sam removes only one of his shoes and hobbles to make Barbara laugh. They begin walking again, holding each other's hands.

A bird swoops low toward them and up again toward the village on the green seaside hill. Sam skips after the bird. Barbara wants to chase after him, but her senses wander toward the sea as Sam disappears behind a large rock.

Barbara stops to reach for a seashell. Her dress drapes to the wet sand she grabs with her toes, like in a fist. The small waves ebb beneath her. She picks up a shell and muses, "He's gone to fetch me flowers and he will bring them to me, trembling, because he's run so far to get them." Barbara closes her eyes and replaces the seashell. "They will be exotic flowers, flowers no one has ever seen." She giggles because of her thoughts of him. His absence makes her long for him.

Barbara stands and slowly steps toward the rock counting the months in the sand he will be gone. "Behind the rock," she imagines Sam trapped in a gigantic web. A spider the size of the unexplainable universe could have its fangs over him. "It could turn on me. But," she thinks how gallantly Sam would slay the spider and that he would never let it hurt her.

She swings her shoes and the cool air passes

through the cold seawater in her dress. She can feel Sam's absent hand in hers. She calls to him.

Sam jumps out from behind the rock and above – landing ankle deep in the sand. He has tried to scare Barbara but with only half of his heart and with a smile on his face.

"Where did you go?" Barbara says.

Wrapping his arms around her he looks out – past the sea – and says, "It is nowhere I have been." Yet, he thinks, to where from here? It is the journey of the man to make and the life of a woman to care.

They know not what keeps them, pressed there, against their bodies, their bodies.

"The endless sea."

They look into each other's eyes and see beyond the future. They are comfortable, uncomfortably knowing, nothing is certain.

She says, "To breakfast then! We'll have waffles with fresh *strawberries*."

'I don't like *strawberries*,' he says with a delicate look and she, '*I know*', with hers.

"For you," Barbara says. "I have been hiding a melon in the shed to ripen it and today is the day you will eat it."

Sam smiles and says, "Yes. Today is the day. And I am a man and you are a woman and the sea is the sea and the rock is the painted rock."

"And we will be happy forever."

"Yes, forever."

"Yes."

Five Poems *(Post Katrina)*
—Dennis Formento

Note: During the spring of 2005 Sam Abrams contacted me about his planned trip to New Orleans. A few months later, Hurricane Katrina, human ineptness and greed conspired to destroy the Gulf Coast and its queen city. He never made the trip, but I know what he would say if he had come here.

Let my people come home
(or What Would Sam Abrams Say?)

pump fire, flood,
famine, blood
into our houses,
wail from our roofs

and get shafted

my whole head is dilating
o eye of eyes
*

they do what they will tho they
know it is wrong, to be
smart about it

simile as raw fact:
the ancient pyramids seethed
like a hole in the ground

what a pity the rain
hasn't washed away the ruins

and the neighborhood,
good god,
has sadly died away

ignorance is blisters
man's inanity to man

the silence of road kill

since yesterday
a hawk squashed
on the US 11 bridge
one wing fanning the wind

Post-K haiku

Alligator hide
made out of a tire
on the roadside

the silence of road kill, part ii

Rotten pelts of nutria
on the road
a length of dead hose
that is a snake
cats and dogs
out of place on
a roadway cut
out of a swamp
a truck turned ass
backwards into
the road
its nose
pointed square into
your headlights
its tail falling
into the pit

is that a black dog or
a busted tire
a rusted bike
left out on
the interstate
to die

Spring Song
for Sam Abrams

wasp hovering
at my back window,
finches gold
down turned
on the feeder

so warm last night,
we opened the bedroom
windows
to sleep.

Train song coming
through the blinds
saying cargo's going back
into New Orleans.

No Money in Art
—Mark Maslow

There is no "M" in art
MTV
Manufactured Music
Selling art as popular as new
Selling art as a product
Like Processed Cheese
Selling art because the artist is pretty
Selling art because it is safe for children
Safety wrapped shrink
to keep unwanted freedom from getting in
Clear
to let the visions of low-grade carbon intelligence out
There is no "M" in art

There is no "O" in art
Opinions only objective on official letterhead
Only justified by random letters
found after a name
or on pieces of vellum framed on the walls
of cubic offices
OBJECTIONABLE MATERIAL FOUND
MEDIA ALERTED
Artist
Terrorist
Victim on mass damnation
This DAMN NATION
DAMN POPULACE
DAMN INNOVATION
DAMN DARWIN DAMN FREEDOM
Only safe art allowed
Dictated

by dollars and cents
Dictated
by endowments, contracts, deals
made only with
safe, controllable artists.

Combustion flames fires long held in check
poker stoking long cold embers

There is no "N" in art
Nightmares never need to be known
Now new nothings made famous
by happy anger slants on old emotions
The edge is never blurred always sharp
dagger balanced tip on the lever of destiny
bounded on all sides with endless green.
Rehash the old: Fall to green
Remix the old: Fall to green
Reinterpret the old: Fall to green
The three 'R's of success
Rehash, Remix and Roll over
Accept the cock media prick shoved down your throat
for your greater good
No Couch.
Not Rape.
No Roofies.
This is "Career Advancement"
A laundry to wash clean the art.

There is no "E" in art
Even Elvis eventually succumbed
to the high-torr environment
To keep his hunger abated

To feed Maple Syrup cherries to old housewives
To keep elapsed minutes moving slowly
Dragging snail slime trails on cement bricks
walked long ago
walked daily by unknowns fragile
shelled for scraps of coin and backdoors
for bones or craps to garner life's needs
Boulevard's broken down
Broken pavement. Cracks travel.

There is no "Y" in art
No big philosophies questioned
No theories
No new worlds, Brave or Old
Nothing New
Rehashed, Retooled, Regurgitated
Pop Menace eating Pop's excrement
Don't be different
Don't be unique
Sound the same Sound
Similar
Sound like yesterday's hits
There is no MONEY in art
There is no living to be made on the edge of civilization
Resampled and purified by the cong(lomerate)s
repackaged for the masses with dictated opinions
Peer-Pressured at the human level
Engineered using statistics and trends
If only all were as honest as the Spice Girls

There is no MONEY in art
There is no MONEY in art
There is no MONEY in art!

REVISION
—Leah Zazulyer

Her Father's Father, the Torah scribe,
(God forbid a mistake!)
was once sold disappearing ink.
He fled on a journey of penance,
wandering worn and wan
until absolved by pneumonia
somewhere at thirty.

Her Father, Yud, Yud Segal, the Yiddish poet,
(God forbid a mistake!)
also revered the ink on paper.
The penance of revision
he journeyed by brain,
the only way he knew
always to come home.

CAFÉ, CINCINNATI AIRPORT
—Leah Zazulyer

Overly solicitous kid waiter
recommends the quesadillas
and made to order chocolate chip
cookies—not as great as his mother's
but darn good.

How are things—four times
more water, like lemon—three times
extra napkins—five supplied
your flight on time?

Just back from Iraq, he boasts
where he learned a lot and
was proud to serve his country
in a tech support van near Basra.

Combat I ask—
not really, just saw wounded
in the field hospital and
promised my dying buddy
to tell his mother goodbye.

We are against the war I venture;
well yeah, you know he says—
crouching now beside our booth
as if taking cover in a fox hole—
in my poli-sci class at junior college
our teacher used to say it was all about oil
and I listen a lot when Bush was running
that first time against—I forgot his name,
but it was hard to figure, and finally

I decided every president wants the best
they just have different ways...

So how're the cookies he asks—
its melted chocolate bleeding all over my hands—
my 26th birthday is coming up
and mom's promised to make me some,
I can hardly wait.

Imaginary Sam
—Frank Judge

There's no road to the towns &
cities of memory. Roads vanish
without a trace. You remember one way,
scraps of paper say it was another.

But so what? It was August.
I'd got a summer tan on black Italian sand
polishing off Roth (*Our Gang*) &
Mailer (*An American Dream*),
the 60s dying fast on us,
though we wouldn't hear of it.

We formed a vague circle, half facing
the blaring tube at Shreela Ray's house
on Dartmouth, the closest
to a salon we had.
It was years before her night conversations,
years before cigarette
after cigarette made a difference.

We sat on floor pillows, beanbags,
a white keyhole wicker chair, as
Mark Spitz took his 7 Munich medals,
Shreela cheering with the lust of a teenager.

"This is Sam," she declared to me,
an arm sweeping the air
over part of the room, eyes flickering
from the thrill of victory for a full 5 seconds.
"Our new neighbor...From New York....
He's a poet *too*....an editor... You two
should get to know each other."

We talked lit mags, politics, Whitman –
Spitz replaying in the background –
over beer, pop, chips, pot. There must
have been wine & cheese – there
always was. And incense.

Sam of the New York poets, of St. Mark's,
of Carroll, di Prima, Blackburn, O'Hara,
Oppenheimer, Ginsberg – names
he could recite like beads on a rosary,
a prayer to go with each one.

I'd met most of them. Even my summer read,
Mailer, via the son of a friend of an uncle.
Saw the same mad hair, the same
committed, combative eyes gleaming back
across Shreela's wine and chaos.

Death never felt at our shoulders then,
though Black September turned the Olympics gray
though the war ground on, though friends
never returned from the jungle dark.
The women, the drugs, the music – everything
was still almost possible. Watergate was
just over the horizon; a Decider & Patriot Acts
just wet dreams for Tricky Dick & J. Edgar.

But what did I know?
Fresh from a Fulbright, set to teach
at the clean campus of polished brick
Il Duce would have loved, I wondered.
"Watch out!" Sam whispered forcefully,
a tipsy old mariner with news from many ports of call.

"It's not safe to have a solid base
in a place like that. Keep your eyes
off the bricks. They're tricky. Keep writing."

He was right. Not much good comes
of so much symmetry. The real writing
almost stopped.
This was years before the CIA cover broke,
before Old Pothead, Athens, Crete,
the bronze tan of a Prospero in semi-retirement.

Years passed. I wrote again.
Wrote Shreela. No reply.
Phoned. Disconnected.
The cigarettes caught her at last. Her face remains
staring from the dark Dustbook cover,
her voice still singing.
I phoned Sam. Disconnected.
But still alive the web shot back
with its illusory assurance.
Was he still at the front, raging
that his country, Walt's country,
would have to be taken back
from our own, sleepers in our midst
who'd passed as us and we'd dismissed?
His site, years out of date, still declared
"Don't believe a word I say! Check it out!"

Either way, he was right. Some day
I'll check to see if there's an island
where he rules and works his farm, recites Walt
to visitors, and writes poems deep into the night.

Sam and the Oysters
—Larry Belle (Nov. 5, 2006)

It was the late Seventies and the big stuff was over and done with, just fresh memories. The Civil Rights Movement had spawned its own establishment. The Vietnam War was on its way to becoming a memorial. The Kennedys, King and Johnson were dead. Watergate ended the opportunity to kick Nixon around. "We Shall Overcome" was sung with more nostalgia than conviction.

But people still knew about, some even read, Marshall McLuhan, Ram Dass, and Bucky Fuller. And the *Whole Earth Catalogue*, our wish book, still offered sweet comfort after a bad day of teaching or a faculty meeting.

Sam came to RIT determined to infuse RIT, an unmistakably careerist institution, with some of the spirit of Allen Ginsberg and a New Hampshire commune. He invited subversive poet friends to do readings he paid for by begging funds from anyone he knew, or sort of knew, with access to a campus budget.

After a reading or on a random Friday night, Sam and Barbara would gather a collection of faculty friends, a visiting poet, perhaps a community activist or two, and select graduate and undergraduate students, into the folds of their living room. We would smoke, drink cheap wine, eat Barbara's good food, and talk about creeping fascism in the RIT College of Liberal Arts administration, along with the esthetic and nutritional failure of twentieth-century American commercial culture; this was a standard academic ritual of the 1970's performed in faculty ghettos from Cambridge to Berkeley.

    Sam was a member of our neighborhood RIT car pool that included Gordon, Stan, Wiley and from time to time Sue and Pat. Sam and I hardly considered the day worth starting without a vigorous argument about politics, culture or the state of the world. Sam would take the Marxist-anarchist position. I, being a member of the Quisling class, a university administrator, would generally defend what I would call the moderate-rationalist position. He was Trotsky; I was Kissinger. But our respective ideologies, though consistently and sincerely held, were not the most important thing. What was most important was the argument. We were like two dogs just getting up and doing our morning stretches.

    Probably our most memorable and vigorous argument ever was over whether fresh seafood, particularly clams and oysters, were more readily available in Rochester at the end of the nineteenth century or now, and when available whether they were tastier then or now. Sam held that that in the 1890s and well into the early years of the twentieth century, Atlantic oysters and clams were packed in ice and daily rushed to Rochester by swift steam engines and were thus certainly better than anything currently available. I, on the other hand, stoutly defended the present and modern technology. I held that with a combination of refrigerated trucks and air transportation plus modern refrigerated display cases, seafood, notably oysters and clams, were bound to be fresher and tastier now than they were then.

The question remained unresolved, and like our friendship, has endured for thirty years.

Sam
—Dane Gordon

Unpredictable, irrepressible
but predictably irrepressible
and irrepressibly busting
with ideas.
Sometimes they're improbable
even impossible,
yet always a kernel
of what we'd call good sense.
It may take some finding
when people don't know
his way.
Unpredictable, irrepressible
but predictably kind:
an irrepressibly good
colleague.

For Sammy
—Mark Price

"Swing to the left;
Swing to the right;
Stand up, sit down,
Fight, fight, fight!"

Anonymous football cheer—c. 1960

SWING TO THE LEFT;
NOT TO THE RIGHT;
NEVER SIT DOWN,
FIGHT, FIGHT, FIGHT!

MARCH WITH THE POOR;
BE THEIR NEW LIGHT;
NEVER SIT DOWN,
FIGHT, FIGHT, FIGHT!

RAIL AT THE WARS;
AT GOVERNMENTS' MIGHT;
NEVER SIT DOWN,
FIGHT, FIGHT, FIGHT!

SHELTER OUR WATER,
OUR TREES, OUR DELIGHT,
NEVER SIT DOWN,
FIGHT, FIGHT, FIGHT!

WRITE THE GOOD POEM,

BLESSED WITH YOUR LIGHT,
NEVER SIT DOWN,
FIGHT, FIGHT, FIGHT!

STAY ON THE LEFT,
DISTRUST THE RIGHT;
ALWAYS STAND TALL:
FIGHT,

- FIGHT,
FIGHT!

Love Mark Price 2005

"I See You, Sojourner . . ."
A Meditation for Sam
—Mary Lynn Broe (May 12, 2005)

In late summer, 2002, Sam Abrams and I got acquainted one afternoon in Java Wally's coffee shop. Together we reverenced the monster, Charles Henri Ford, bad boy of The Dakota and Hanya, Crete—at that time, I was still Charles' executor-- and a number of other American poets and expatriates. Grizzled, curmudgeonly, always belovedly political, he had been layering the RIT terrain with his infamous S(P)AM email. He had just published *Old Pothead* poems. A year later, Sam would bring a grievance against me as chair of his department.

>Remembering our paths of conversation,
>I see you, sojourner, armed with an
>old leather backpack,
>scuffed by years of travel and
>loving stuffed with
>this nourishment for your journeys,
>Wayfarer:
>
>a grainy vinyl recording of the *Virgin Fugs*
>
>a toast of Absinthe from the
>Boeuf sur le Toit, Paris, 1921
>
>a crumbled newspaper clipping recounting
>Dorothy Day's fistfight with Emily Holmes Coleman
>at the Catholic Worker, Tivoli, New York
>in the late thirties.

a well-worn copy of Edward Dahlberg's
Sorrows of Priapus

a couple of stones from Devil's Bathtub,
Mendon Ponds' Park

Strains of Slam Stewart, humming,
jamming with Benny Goodman at
Eddie Condon's, Avenue C (or is it Avenue A?)
leak from the pack

a crumpled parchment bookmark,
stuck in your poems, reads:
"*Liber, caris eris Romae,
donec te deserat aetas:
aut tineas pasces taciturnus inertes,
aut poeros elementa docens manes.*"

*(Book, if you're lucky you'll be loved in Rome;
if you're unlucky, you'll be chewed by bookworms
and forgotten;
if you're very unlucky
you might become a textbook.)*
Horace, Epistulae, I, 20.

Folded into a pocket,
close to the skin,
you keep this worn Whitman poem:

"*I hear it was charged against me that I sought to
                                      destroy
Institutions, but really, I am neither for nor against
                                        institutions
(What indeed have I in common with them? or

what with the destruction of them?)
Only I will establish in the Mannahatta and in every
city of these states inland and seaboard,
And in the fields and woods, and above every keep
little or large that dents the water,
Without edifices or rules or trustees or any
argument,
The institution of the clear love of comrades."

Be on your way, friend,
godspeed and goodwill.

I forgive you all your trespasses though
You did not forgive me mine.

(When I finished my tribute to him that day of his retirement party, Sam lifted his head: "How could someone I've never slept with have gotten me so right?")

he ain't no punk
(for Sam Abrams)
—vincent f. a. golphin

he grabs mine
so i latch onto his
soul mirror
we swirl
eyes to eyes
mind to mind
rams on a mountain slope
head to head
across a table
head to head
we wrestle
in fascination
in familiarity
in testosterone fling
like Jacob
i hold on
until he blesses me
i'd hate to play poker against you
he says with a smile
i once played with Baraka
respect
i walk away
and say silently
he ain't no punk

Don't Die, Sam
—Graham Mackenzie

Please don't die, Sam
Not any time soon;
Least not before me, anyway

All angsty, thinking of what
I'll say at yr funeral
(I'm sure you're not surprised)

Standing at the lectern
Room as quiet as black
Din as murmur as warm

Stuffy with people so not
They all knew you well
Before me, so well

Plus, you're standing over me
As always as I speak
As I type as I think

As I read I have only myself
To blame for putting you there
Where you gladly went

A lecture machine I didn't
Even need to put a quarter in
Lecturing the corn in Illinois

You know what gives
The lie? Your inconsistency
Is totally consistent

Fuck the prudes
I, for one, can't
Help but love you

FUCK IT, SAM
—Peter Ferran

I read here, in an Academic Conference Prospectus,
that
My recently acquired colleague
Sam
    Who composes poetry
    Who does Whitman
    Who knew Ginsberg
    Who quirkily challenges his Liberal Arts
colleagues to own up
        (to what, they don't know)

Dropped out of Academia [sic] from 1968 to 1978!!

Well, he missed the Real Action.

In that crux decade
The Truly Retributive events went down:
    Recanting of radical politics
    Reconstitution of liberal stanchions
    Reconstruction of staunch opinions
    Revamping of capitalist tactics

= "Retrenchment"

(But there was no
    Recalling [elected] officials / [installed]
    Retracting [imbecilic ideas] / [rooted policies]
    Remanding done deals
    . . .)

And what did I, Sam's kindred spirit
Do while Sam was out?

Got PhD in Comp Lit
Resolved to Change the World
Taught for the Big U
Played Jazz
Progressed towards Tenure
Smoked a little Grass
Got screwed inside the System

Said "Fuck it"

Couldn't make it stick

   Should've done what Sam did.

For Sam Abrams
—Jack Bradigan Spula

Every year I plant a gift
To the spirits of my backyard, the ones that come and go
Disguised as cats, rabbits, sometimes a woodchuck or raccoon,
A squadron of crows, a lone blue jay —
All the disguises that the soul has wrought
With considerable pain and ecstasy
From a billion years of chemical agitation
And alignment.
But the gift? Every year it's a small evergreen.
That's the beginning and end of it. If I had religion,
I'd make claims for the little potted tree
That I select each December, but the fact is,
It's only a spruce or fir or pine,
Whatever has been left unsold at the nursery
On that last night open, before calm arrives
With the shortest day.
But never mind its curvature and thin crown: this tree is a
Monument in the making. It could have been a poem
But wasn't so lucky.
And so I will dig the hole to specifications, and I will
Treat the roots, even down to the root hairs, like
The spirits they must be. But this year, I will add
A thought about a poet and friend and comrade,
With plain gratitude. I can almost hear
The roots digging deeper at the thought.

Contributors Notes

Amiri Baraka: Newest book TALES OF THE OUT & THE GONE (Akashic); <u>Dutchman</u> revival just closed in NYC Cherry Lane. Met Sam & Barbara in The Village when the Cedar Tavern was the ultimate waterhole, and we wd meet weekends with Joel Oppenheimer, Gil Sorrentino, Joe Early, AB Spellman, Max Finstein, Fielding Dawson & ad infi to discuss poetry and the world.

Larry Belle earned his Ph.D. in medieval and Renaissance history at the University of Rochester. For thirty years at RIT he was a utility infield administrator. Among other jobs, he served as director of instructional development, assistant vice president for faculty and program development and dean of the College of Continuing Education.

Glenn Bewley is a Former student of Sam's, now living in Tennessee.

Alan Boegehold: Julie and I met Sam and Barbara in Champaign-Urbana IL in 1958. We quickly discovered that we found the same things funny, and now almost fifty years later, we still do.

Mary Lynn Broe: As his department chair, I knew Sam from 2002-2005. We often traded wild stories about American expatriate friends in common. Together we entered the "zoomorphic circle" in our abiding love for dogs.

My name is **Vivianna Calabria**, one of Sam's students from '97-'98. An anecdote starring Sam: Sam is an old Jewish guy from my parents' Brooklyn neighborhood; my parents are both Italian/Sicilian and always had Jewish friends. As a family, we tend to gravitate toward people who turn out be from their neighborhood. When I came to RIT, fate had it that my two favorite professors, and the ones with whom I'd stay in touch with for the long haul, were Jewish guys from Brooklyn.

Sam knows the Verrazzano Bridge, he knows Bay Ridge, he knows 86th Street, he knows Italians, and he was entertained by a tale from my childhood of our family being in hour-long halted traffic on the lower level of the VB while the New York City Marathon runners crossed the top level. The entire bridge was shaking up and down unforgettably.

I love Sam dearly, and I also love his wife, who helped me change a flat when she was extremely hard of sight following an operation.

I love you, Professore! In bocca al lupo

Andrei Codrescu: I met Sam when I attended his first St. Marks Poetry Project class at the Old Courthouse on Second Avenue in New York in 1968. Sam made everyone smoke a joint, which made me feel very weird during his lecture and I couldn't read my poems in English -- pot always made me super-conscious of my accent. So I went to Ted Berrigan's speedy benzedrine class, which was a lot more to my liking. Later I re-met Sam and got to know him at his and Barbara's apartment across the street from the St. Marks' Church -- he gave me a copy of his Olympia Press porn novel, "Barbara."

Jim Cohn is the director of the online Museum of American Poetics (http://www.poetspath.com). A postbeat era master poet, he studied under Corso, Snyder, Whalen, Waldman at Naropa Institute where he served as teaching assistant for Allen Ginsberg in 1980. Meeting Sam Abrams after moving to Rochester in 1982 served as an East Coast watershed. Through Sam one got to know Creeley, Sanders, Oppenheimer, Rakosi, Baraka, Blackburn. Before there was Gonzo, there was Sam taking on the Academy over Whitman. Before there was ecopoetics, there he was, tracing things back to their origins. In 1984, while a student at NTID studying American Sign Language, Sam offered critical assistance to Cohn in arranging a Deaf-Beat Summit featuring Deaf poet Robert Panara and Mr. Ginsberg. In 2007, they read together at St. Marks Poetry Project.

Joe Early: At 13 heard Bird & entered a different &, I thought, richer culture. Then the US sent me off to Europe, to Raphael, Rembrandt. On it went, Cezanne, Monet, Kline, Guston. Fortuitous friendship with Tony Weinberger led to an intense reading of Doc Bill, EzPo &, later, Stevens, Reznikoff. The composer Frank Busto guided me to Bach, Beethoven, Bartok. Now, the Bronx kiddo is on a bargain gold coast. Viva music, art, poetry & grazia a Marcella Hazan!

Peter Ferran: I met Sam Abrams when I joined the faculty of RIT's College of Liberal Arts in 1993, and I immediately swore silent allegiance to his dedication to upsetting his complacent faculty colleagues through constant ironic representations of their foibles.

Karen E. Fields: I met Sam through his brother, Jerry, my attorney in Massachusetts. As I was leaving for a position at the University of Rochester, Jerry told me to get in touch with his brother and sister-in-law. "You'll love them," he said. I did.

Dennis Formento: I read Sam's book on Walt Whitman and dug it, so Sam sent me poems for *Mesechabe: The Journal of Surregionalism*. Sam immediately invited me to visit his house on Crete, but I ain't never made it. "Next year, in Chania!"

Vincent F. A. Golphin is on the Rochester Institute of Technology English faculty, as was Sam Abrams. His latest poetry collection is *Like A Dry Land: A Soul Journey Through the Middle East* (Foothills, 2006).

Dane Gordon: Professor of Philosophy in College of Liberal Arts (now retired) so a colleague of Sam. Author of several books on philosophy and theology as well as a history of RIT.

Bob Holman owes Sam a whole lot -- Sam was the first of the previous generation poets who "got it," what was coming out the Nuyorican Poets Cafe, the birth of slam and perf and hip hop poesy, and invited us ALL up to Rochester where one poet, Mike Tyler, borrowed Sam's DEA (Drug Enforcement Agency) jacket to go to the store, got busted (drawn guns et al), the poem goes on from there (to Chania) -- and the time Sam read Baudelaire at the Dead Poets Slam at the Nuyorican (he lost)....

Frank Judge is a longtime Rochesterian. He is Editor and Publisher of *Exit Online* and the *Pinnacle Hill Review* and is currently President of Rochester Poets and Director of the Rochester Poetry Workshop. Since 2004, he has also been the Rochester area organizer for Poets Against the War & Occupation, and, in March of 2006 served as a coordinator for the first Western New York World Poetry Day Festival.

Diane Katsiaficas: We met in Greece when he and Barbara were there on a Fulbright in 1990-91 and have tendered the friendship over the years.
As you may know, Sam loves the sea. olives. and almost all things

George Kimball retired last year after a quarter-century spent as a sports columnist for the Boston Herald. A past recipient of the Nat Fleischer Award for Distinguished Boxing Journalism, he continues to write the weekly 'America at Large' column for Dublin's *Irish Times* and is a columnist for *TheSweetScience.com*. His latest book, *Chairman of the Boards* (co-authored by Eamonn Coghlan) will be published in 2007 by Red Rock Press in Ireland. He lives in New York City with his wife, the psychiatrist Marge Marash.

Tuli Kupferberg is an American counterculture poet, author, cartoonist, anarchist, and publisher and co-founder of the band *The Fugs*. He lives in NYC.

Mark Maslow was challenged by Sam Abrams from 1994-1996 and still feels his influence. Maslow has taken his poetry across the US and Europe. He has been hosting and supporting poetry in Austin, TX since 1998 and has been the host of the Ruta Maya Open Mic Poetry (www.freespeechart.com) series since early 1999.

Graham Arthur Mackenzie, born Jan. 12, 1977, Columbia S.C. Musician, philosopher, poet, scientist, mathematician (proGrammar.net). Professional American Sign Language Interpreter and Educational Futurist (ExplainingConcepts.com). Met Sam taking a poetry class of his at RIT, education continued outside of classroom.

Larry Meyers: I'm on the English Department faculty at Hunter College in New York, where my wife and I live. I was active in the 60s in civil rights and pro-Castro politics in Ann Arbor, and in anti-Vietnam war efforts in San Francisco and New York. I currently oppose the Iraq war and demonstrate against it. My formal name is Lewis Meyers.

Mark Price is an Emeritus Professor of English at RIT, where he was Sam's colleague for many years, and, like Sam, an Advisor to *Signatures* Magazine.

John Retallack is a Colleague of Sam's at RIT, where he teaches Photography and chairs the Visual Media Department.

Bob Rixon (a.k.a. DJ Rix): I was a student of joel oppenheimer in the 70s. I didn't actually meet Sam until after joel died, & that was serendipity.

John Roche teaches English at RIT, and counts Sam Abrams as one of his mentors. He teaches a number of classes Sam used to teach, including Walt Whitman and Creative Writing, and advises the student magazine Sam started, *Signatures*.

Ed Sanders has known Sam Abrams since NYC in the 1960s where Ed ran the Peace Eye Bookstore and formed The Fugs. He visited Sam's last poetry class at RIT in 2004.

Greg Slater: I was Sam's student during my Undergraduate studies 87-91. I share a natural love of, poetry and Good Bud. I also was his tenant for a short stint on Harvard street. I greatly appreciate his dedication and talent plus his indomitable spirit!

Joel Sloman: Poet, born in Brooklyn in 1943. Assistant Director of Poetry Project 1966-1967. Books: *Virgil's Machines* (1966), *Stops* (1997), *Cuban Journal*

Benjamin North Spencer is the founding editor of NorthernPros.com and *Cadillac Cicatrix*. He has been a member of the Writers Workshop at the University of Iowa and is a graduate of the Jack Kerouac School of Disembodied Poetics at Naropa University. His novel *Godspeed on the Beggars at Dawn* was featured at the Unpublished Underground Gallery in New York in 2005. He is a member of the Monterey County Film Commission. Spencer lives and works in Carmel Valley, California where he is currently doing research for a novel about the wine industry.

Jack Bradigan Spula is a Rochester-based writer, pianist, teacher and activist; he's worked with Sam since the heady days of the Citizens Party (1980) and looks forward to standing alongside him on the much-needed pickets and protests ahead. He is a journalist, activist, and editor of *The Rochester Dissident* jackbradiganspula.tripod.com.

M. G. Stephens attended workshops at the St. Mark's Poetry Project in the late 1960s, including one offered by Sam Abrams. It was Sam who first encouraged Mick to write prose for The World, the monthly mimeo magazine at the Poetry Project. Mick went on to write eighteen books, most of them prose, including Season at Coole and The Brooklyn Book of the Dead. He recently was awarded a PhD from the University of Essex in Colchester, England, with a thesis on the St. Mark's Poetry Project. He has lived in London for the past five and half years.

Anne Waldman: Sam and I worked in the same poetry zones at The Poetry Project in the early years when Joel Oppenheimer was heading up the "outrider" vision. I admired his political work and wit, his "Greek" cynic's sharp tongue. We stayed connected over the ensuing years. I remember being hosted by him in Rochester close to Robert Duncan's death, and have a wonderful sense of his generosity as teacher, scholar & poet.

Tony Weinberger quit NYC for Vermont at the end of the 60s--publishing had become a mugs' game. Retired from race car fabrication and hydro-electric turbine erection at the end of the 90s. Now travels the competitive trapshooting circus. The winnings are chump change, but the silver buckles are swell.

Leah Zazulyer: A teacher/school psychologist, poet/writer, translator/from Yiddish, with a fourth book soon to be published by FootHills Publishing. Long interested in issues pertaining to the interface between culture and language, I grew up in California, with parents from Belarus, and came to Rochester in 1968.

 I'm still discovering Sam—the hip writer/professor who dared to bring Amira Baraka to Rochester, the "Lamed-Vovnik" disguised as a good neighbor to poet Shreela Ray, the lover of classical and contemporary Greece willing to share his lore...May he continue in retirement and peace to discover himself!